Forty-Five Letters
FROM A WORLD WAR II SAILOR

Forty-Five Letters
FROM A WORLD WAR II SAILOR

*How to Fulfill
Your American Dreams*

EDITED BY ROBERT W. BRADSHAW

FORTY-FIVE LETTERS FROM A WORLD WAR II SAILOR
HOW TO FULFILL YOUR AMERICAN DREAMS

iUniverse books may be ordered through booksellers or by contacting:

iUniverse
1663 Liberty Drive
Bloomington, IN 47403
www.iuniverse.com
1-800-Authors (1-800-288-4677)

ISBN: 978-1-4917-7185-3 (sc)
ISBN: 978-1-4917-7186-0 (e)

Library of Congress Control Number: 2015913405

Print information available on the last page.

iUniverse rev. date: 09/23/2015

Contents

Introduction

Frank B. Bradshaw Jr. (1926–1996) was born in Memphis, Tennessee, and received his college education from Cornell University, graduating from Cornell Engineering College in three years. He served in World War II as a sailor in the US Merchant Marine Corps, during which time he wrote forty-five letters to his "Dearest Mother and Daddy." He served in the Cold War as a US Air Force officer in the Special Weapons Command at Manzano Base, southeast of Sandia, which currently provides counterterrorism response for weapons of mass destruction.

The purpose of *Forty-Five* is to honor the memory of my father, Frank B. Bradshaw Jr., for students of American history and for students of American dreams, thereby illustrating a son's love for his family and country so that future generations will have a road map to fulfill their dreams.

This is a story of a sailor in World War II.

Letter 1
Pass Christian, Mississippi, USA
December 21, 1944

Love for Family
Love for Country

Dear Mother and Daddy, Ann, and Charlie,

I'm a pretty poor excuse as a letter writer, but I guess you all will just have to put up with me. I've had good intentions of writing for the last three nights, but it's just one thing after another, so I haven't gotten it done.

For the last three days, they've worked our heads off. Tomorrow we're going on a trip on the ocean all day long, and we're really looking forward to it.

It's not any use talking about it, and I might have done the wrong thing by not coming home Christmas, but you all can just remember

I'll be thinking about you all and wishing I was with you. I'd rather be there than any place on earth. Tell everyone hello for me at the Christmas Eve dinner and I wish I could be there to see them all.

Love you all,
Frank

This is for Mother, Ann, and Charlie, and I'll fix Daddy up when I get home.

Letter 2
New Orleans, Louisiana, USA
March 5, 1945

Love for Family
Love for Country

Dearest Mother and Daddy,

Got here with all my baggage and had it all checked at the train station except one bag. The train was approximately on time.

The biggest change in the weather took place when we were in about the middle part of Mississippi. I imagine you can guess that it became about twenty degrees hotter all of a sudden. It is really hot here in New Orleans.

I got a room at the Roosevelt, and the room is really nice. It cost a little more, but it was the only one I could get here.

I ate a couple of meals on the train, and much to my astonishment, they were good. The train I came down on was clean, and no coal peeped into the coaches.

Everything so far is going fine, and tomorrow at nine, I'll find out the news. I'll reach you before this letter though. I'm sure.

I didn't tell you all exactly how much my stay at home meant to me, and I'll never forget how much both of you did for me. Thanks so much for my wonderful home stay.

Love you,
Frank

Letter 3
Savannah, Georgia, USA
March 9, 1945

Dear Mother and Daddy,

Today we haven't been doing much except signing the ship's articles. There are some papers everybody on board has to sign before going on a trip. We have moved a few miles up the river this morning and into dry dock. We had four tugboats pulling us.

I've been helping the chief with the crew when they sign the articles. When they would want to make an allotment or take out insurance, I would fill it out.

To get to the ship, we have to ride a boat across the river. It is operated by the steamship line, so it does not cost anything to ride it.

We have a lifesaving suit apiece, a helmet, a life jacket, a whistle, and a light attached to the life preserver. There are three former cadets on the ship that are now in the crew; they seem to be good boys.

I forgot to tell you we had a rug on the floor also. Another good thing is that we have a laundry aboard.

The food so far has been excellent. Two or three meats for every meal, three or four vegetables, dessert, drinks. They have waiters and fresh white tablecloths for every meal. We have a separate menu for every meal and can order what we want.

Twice a day, at ten and three, everybody knocks off work and observes coffee time for fifteen minutes.

All of the officers that I've met so far have been extra nice. The captain reminds me very much of Papa. When I was making those allotments, he came in, sat down by me, and had a friendly little chat. He asked me a bunch of little questions.

In our room, we have two good bunks, a leather couch, a double deck, washbasin, two closets, four big drawers built in, bed lights on the beds, and four other lights in the room. In floor space, it is not so very big, but it is compact, neat, and nice. Containing everything we need.

I've been up and down the ship and in and out and still haven't been all over it by a long shot. This is the only place I've ever really gotten lost. I get turned around and don't know the bow from the stern when I start walking in all the hallways. Better go now.

Love always,
Frank

Letter 4
Savannah, Georgia, USA
March 11, 1945

Dear Mother and Daddy,

It is now Sunday about twelve thirty, and we have just eaten dinner. Had a very good dinner: roast, barbecue chicken, soup, salad, potatoes, spinach, asparagus, coffee, tea, or milk, and peach pie with ice cream. Pretty good, eh!

So far, I haven't done any manual labor and just a little work in the chart room, and also this morning, I checked some cargo that came aboard.

We have moved from dry dock and are now at a warehouse getting the ship's stores. It will take two days for us to stock the ships, and it is pretty definite we will leave for Cuba to get our cargo next Tuesday.

The officers here on the ship are as nice as anyone could ask for. Practically everyone—except the captain—graduated from the academy, and all have offered to help me as much as they could.

If I get tired, I can go take a nap. So far, they don't just give me an order, but ask me if I would like to do some little jobs with them.

Every morning about nine or ten, I go to the chief mate's room and copy the rough log into the smooth log. This only takes about fifteen minutes. Then yesterday afternoon, I helped the third mate check the lifeboats and life rafts.

When we shift from one place to another, it is very interesting to watch the tug maneuver the ship.

We have changed places three times, so I have been on the bow, the bridge, and the stern during the three different times to see what each mate does.

The captain is a very rich man; he has some oil wells in Oklahoma.

The steward cleans up our room every morning. I don't know if he is supposed to, but he thinks so anyway.

Last night we went to a USO dance in Savannah. It was very good. Again soon.

Love,
Frank

Letter 5
Savannah, Georgia, USA
March 13, 1945

Dearest Mother and Daddy,

I'm going to try to call tonight, but in case the call doesn't get through, I'm going to drop a line.

As the time grows shorter, more rumors fly around the ship. Now it is rumored that we are to go to New York and pick up a cargo of beer and take it to Havana, and get our sugar. I don't think we'll do that. I believe we'll go straight to Havana. The captain had his convoy conference this evening at two thirty and has already gotten the orders where to go. We are pretty definitely not going in a convoy because our ship is too fast. It goes about twenty-five miles per hour, and that is twice as fast as a convoy goes. It usually only goes about ten miles per hour.

We have taken on tons and tons of supplies today, and also we took on three hundred thousand gallons of oil, so we are prepared to go somewhere. We had an abandon-ship drill today, and our lifeboat got way down the river, and we nearly didn't make it back. Finally, we got the motor started and got back.

This morning I copied the smooth log, which took only about twenty minutes. That's one of my jobs every day. For a couple of hours, I watched the stevedores loading the supplies so they wouldn't steal anything. My orders were to hit them with a club if I saw them stealing and ask questions later. They gave me the club, but I was watching them so close none of them tried to get anything.

We have only a couple of more hours' work to do on the motors before we are ready to go. The motors in the ship are gigantic. They are eighty feet high and a hundred feet long. They started them up last night, and the whole ship shook like a baby's cradle.

When we were coming into the dock, the pilot ran the ship into the side of the dock—and tore half the dock down. Well, Ma and Pa and all the rest, I'd better go mail this now, so good-bye for a very short time.

All my love,
Frank

The same time you get this letter, I'll be in Cuba.

Letter 6
Havana, Cuba
March 15, 1945

Educate

Dearest Mother and Daddy,

We arrived early this morning, and this is the most beautiful harbor and city I've ever seen. All the way down, we had good weather, and the sea was very moderate. I didn't feel seasick one bit.

I looked around and asked the pilot who brought us into the harbor if Billy's ship had come in, and he said we were the only

(There were cutouts here—apparently censored.)

The city is huge, and all the buildings are snow white. The temperature early in the morning was eighty, and now at ten thirty, it is above ninety. There were people at the dock selling shoes when we came in and some more there for the laundry, etc.

All the people are speaking Spanish, and I can't understand anything that they are saying.

Coming down, the ocean was more than blue—it was purple. Most of the time, I stayed up on the bridge and sort of helped them.

I didn't get much studying done on this first little trip, because most of the time I stayed outside or did something else.

We are still having very good food, and I think it will continue to be good.

The minute the gangplank was let down, the stevedores poured, and we began to load.

I walked out on the dock, and I've never in all my life seen such greetings—everybody was giving me their card and patting me on the back. I had to run and get back on the ship.

Part of the city is on the side we docked on, but we have to catch a ferry to get to the main part. We're going over about two or four this afternoon.

I like all the officers. The old captain eats just about like Papa—and is just about his size. He knows his stuff about the sea.

This is such a pretty place. You all will have to see it sometime. I really believe you all would like it. I'll write again soon.

Love,
Frank

Letter 7
Havana, Cuba
March 16, 1945

Educate

Dearest Mother and Daddy,

Last night I went into Havana and thought the city was very pretty, but I can't stand these kind of people.

All the buildings are made out of stone by law, and they have a $50 million capitol building. Bands play at open cafés along the sidewalk, and every other establishment is a bar. There are three or four policemen for every block, so many it seems like every other person is a policeman.

The people worry the daylights out of me. All the taxicab drivers follow any Americans down the street and mumble this Spanish all the time.

We're loading very fast, so will probably be out of here in a very short time. I haven't seen Billy's ship yet.

I worked a little bit on my sea project this morning and a little on the mathematics project—but not too much.

As far as work around the ship here, I haven't been doing much except watching the stevedores loading cargo. I check the hold to see if the paper is put down right, and if they break a bag of sugar, I report it. I don't do this but a couple of hours in the morning and evening. Write again soon.

Love always,
Frank

Letter 8
Atlantic Ocean
March 25, 1945

Educate

Dearest Mother and Daddy,

As you can probably guess, we're well on our way now. We've had beautiful weather all the way, and up to now, I haven't been the lightest bit seasick.

The other day, a flying fish flew up on deck and bumped into a winch, killing himself. I got a good look at him, and sure enough, they have wings. We have also seen a couple of whales.

I get up at about five o'clock, go on the bridge, and stay until breakfast at eight o'clock. Then I go back after breakfast for about an hour. All day I am off until after supper, and then I go back and stay a couple of more hours. There's really nothing hard about it.

During the morning, I usually take a nap, then study a little after dinner, and then go play a little ball or something on deck. I'm getting plenty of sleep and plenty to eat. The food is not superb like some fancy restaurant, but it is really good.

The temperature is about the same as in Memphis now, but in the last few days, it has been hotter. We keep our fan going most of the time.

I'm glad I've seen Cuba. The climate is fine—and the scenery is beautiful—but I wouldn't spend very much effort trying to get back. We loaded up in nearly record time. They loaded night and day. So I guess that did the trick.

We're making good speed, but they change our course so often and go so much out of the way that it takes longer than it ordinarily would. When we were off the Florida coast, we saw a bunch of ships all the same, but now we haven't seen one for days.

I never did see Bill before we left Cuba. He must have gone to some other port.

Time seems to pass rapidly. I never know what day it is, but looking back, it seems a long, long time since I was back there, and it's only been three weeks.

We're getting into some trade winds, so the wind has begun to blow fairly hard.

Tell Ann and Charlie I'll write them in a short time. Miss you both.

All my love,
Frank

Letter 9
Atlantic Ocean
March 28, 1945

Love for Family
Love for Country
Educate

Dearest Mother and Daddy,

This is about the tenth day, and we're still going strong. They've changed our course several times, and today, we had orders from over the radio to change our destination. No telling where we'll wind up.

The sea is getting rougher and rougher every day, but the ship rolls easily and we're still riding okay. This seems like the longest trip I've ever taken. It seems like we'll never get there. We're making good time, but there is so much to cover; it naturally takes a little time. The wind has yet to cease blowing.

The cooking and everything about the ship is practically the same as in Savannah. The weather is increasing with cold very slightly.

We passed a life raft the other day, but it was all alone, with no one on it. Every now and then, we pass things like that.

If the water permits, I think I'll try to catch a fish when we anchor. Maybe it'll be a little different from those back there in the old beds of the Mississippi. I'm getting along with my work okay, except the drawings, and I can't make them look like very much. Never could anyway.

I steered a little while last night and held her on a pretty straight course. Must have been beginner's luck. Our room is two decks above the water, and a wave just came in the porthole.

I sure do miss being around home. Really, that was about the longest time since last May. You all made things so nice for me, and it's hard to say how much I enjoyed it.

Love always,
Frank

Letter 10
North Atlantic
March 29, 1945

Dearest Mother and Daddy,

We're close to land today—in fact, close enough to see it very plainly. The Americans made their landing here. Nobody knows what we're going to do. We're just waiting here for orders. The city looks to be about the size of our own.

We tried fishing a little this morning but couldn't catch anything. The land is gentle, rolling slopes, and all of it seems to be in cultivation.

We saw a British sub this morning as we were coming in. We might not be so much alone now from the looks of things around here.

The weather slacked off considerably. Then we got close to land. The harbor is not like the last one. It's just a long beach-like affair, something like Daytona.

While I'm thinking about it, I had better ask you to send me some airmail stamps. We can't get any stamps, and I haven't got any. Send them soon as you can.

Up to now, no one has gone ashore here in this place. We just pulled up and anchored, and not even the captain has gone ashore. We've been here about twelve hours.

This is now March 31.

We're out again and under way. We can see the shoreline practically all the time. The sunsets and sunrises are the most beautiful sights I've ever seen. The weather is good as anyone could ask. The nights are just cool enough to sleep well, and the days warm up considerably. We're running very slow so the other ships can keep up with us. We're the commodore ship.

Twelve Hours Later

The sea today has been like glass.

If you want to do a little map reading, this place we're in is the same latitude that Memphis is in, and the longitude is about eighty-two degrees east of Memphis. Our time is six hours ahead of yours.

Everybody is expecting a peaceful trip. They say there hasn't been much activity over here in a long time. Since all the danger is over, they've cut out all the bonuses, and we won't make very much money. I thought things would be cheaper in other parts, but it is just the opposite.

Everything we did in Havana cost three times as much as it would back home. The people over here are overflowing with money. Everybody has a big roll of bills, even the little boys.

Do you remember the picture and the front of the Prudential life-insurance policy? I have seen one around the house. If you look at that picture, you will see what I saw this morning. Only it doesn't look exactly like that. We can see or could before dark snow-capped mountains on each side of us.

One of my little jobs is to see that the upper two decks are blacked out every night by sunset. Also I have to take down the flag.

The instruments and lights on the bridge and around the ship have to be checked almost every day, so I usually help the mate in checking these. We've cut our speed and are not going like we were at first.

We usually ponder round with that for an hour or so every day and sing some kind of song.

Letter 11
Atlantic Ocean
April 22, 1945

Love for Family
Love for Country
Letters from March 29 to April 22 were either lost or censored.

Dearest Mother and Daddy,

In all probability, I'll get back about the same time this letter arrives—unless we get some order to go some other place. And we're scheduled now; I think we have only one more stop to make.

We've really got the speed and pass everything on the sea. In an hour yesterday, we passed fifteen ships.

The weather is pretty and springlike nearly all the time. Since we've gotten down from the high latitude, it has been extra fine. The wind blows all the time, usually more than twenty miles per hour.

As of now, I haven't been seasick a bit, and I guess I'm over the hump. I'm still doing fine.

In fact, there's not so much for me to do. I get up at five, and go up on the bridge, and stay until eight. Then I go back for a couple of hours at night. During the day, I usually take a nap, read, or piddle around on deck for a while. If there's any question you'd like to ask me, write and do so because everything is getting so natural to me around the ship. I don't know what would be interesting.

We got mail for the first time a couple of days ago, and I got about four letters from you all that were written on March 13 and 20. It was really good to hear how everything was around Memphis and to learn the month-old news. You can't imagine how absorbed and interested I was in those letters.

We are passing some old, old country people who have been around in these parts longer than in any other place.

I was wondering how those pictures turned out we had taken when I was home. Did you ever have a group made or not? That one of Charlie's was such a humdinger. I can see it just as plain now as if I were looking right at it. I guess Elmer is looking at it too! Next time, there'll have to be five made instead of three. Did Ann send Bob a picture?

I don't shave more than once a week; so at times, the beard is rather long. I never have shaved my mustache; so you probably wouldn't recognize me if you saw me.

Having a wide variety and good quality, our food is still okay. We have plenty of fresh fruits and vegetables. We have chicken, steaks, roast beef, and cold cuts for sandwiches in between meals. We have dessert twice a day and fresh bread that is baked every day.

I don't know what we could be doing that is such hard work, because on our ship nobody works very hard. Being new has something to do with this, I imagine. When we get close enough to identify a ship to find out who she is, I'm always looking for the *Wilmington* or the *Sea Carp*, but haven't had any luck up to now.

My officers are still an okay bunch, and we get along fine together.

They have two police and two custom officials on the gangway and on the dock every time that we tie up, so souvenirs are practically taboo. The things in these countries are so rotten.

Did Charlie go on the house party at Easter time? Did you ever see Buford?

I don't know what the regulations are, but if we get into a port on the gulf, I should be able to get home for a day or so. I'll try like the devil anyway.

See you before long.

Love always,
Frank

Letter 12
Baltimore, Maryland, USA
May 6, 1945

Worship
Love for Country
Exposure to Washington, DC, at a Very Early Age

Dearest Mother and Dad,

It is Sunday, and I went to church.

We've finished unloading cargo and are now in dry dock for repair. We are supposed to get repairs until next Saturday.

Saturday, I went to Washington with the radio operator. We saw the Capitol, Washington Monument, National Art Gallery, Smithsonian Institute, National Museum, the different memorials, government buildings, parks, etc. All very interesting and the most beautiful city I've ever seen. Everything was green and blooming.

Since it was Saturday, Congress and the Senate were not in session, so we didn't get to see them. We went down on the train Furlough rater—only cost us a dollar round trip.

Our ship hasn't been given any orders as to where we'll go on our next trip. Everybody, namely the captain, thinks we'll go to Europe. I wish we would go somewhere else. We don't know whether or not we're going to load here in Baltimore. They seem to think we will go to Boston or New York.

Most of the crew is going to stay on the ship, so we'll have a good crew for the next voyage.

I saw Spike Jones and his City Slickers on the stage last night. Really a funny show. We saw a stage show in Washington that was also very good.

I have to take another physical exam before we ship out again. Everybody has to take one; that's a rule they have. We take it at the Baltimore Marine Hospital.

The weather has been cold enough to wear an overcoat every time we go out. It takes about twenty to twenty-five minutes to get to town from where we are located. We are practically at the end of Chesapeake Bay.

I just got the stamps you all sent me. It sure takes a long time for a letter to get to me.

I'll be writing again soon.

Love,
Frank

Letter 13
New York, New York, USA
May 13, 1945

Exposure to New York City at a Very Early Age

Dearest Mother and Dad,

Since this ship is going to be in dry dock for six weeks, I am sure they will take us off and put us on another ship if possible. There is absolutely nothing to do aboard, so we'll be on another ship soon. I still hope I get a cargo ship.

Went on the top of the Empire State Building tonight. Saw all the sights, lights, etc. I got a map of all the subways in New York. Now getting around is easy.

We shifted ships again yesterday but are still in Brooklyn. It only takes about fifteen minutes to get to Times Square from where we are—have to go under East River.

There's not much to Brooklyn, mostly where all the foreigners drift to. Saw the place where the world's fair was, but now it is only decorated buildings.

It won't bother me if they do change us, because I'm about ready to leave this place now. Seen all I want to for a while and would like to go on and make another trip.

We haven't even gone into the dry dock yet.

I'm getting ready to go back up to the cadet office and see if they have any orders for me.

When a new change takes place or more news comes about, I'll let you know.

Love,
Frank

Letter 14
New York, New York, USA
May 17, 1945

SS *Costa Rica Victory*

Dear Mother and Daddy,

I am no longer on the SS *Costa Rica Victory*. Since they are going to convert her, they took me off. I'm waiting here at the cadet office for another ship. About ten boys are ahead of me, so I imagine I'll be here several days. I'm pretty sure to get a tanker this time.

I'm rather disgusted with the way this office performs. Instead of letting me stay on the ship and my pay keep going, they tell me to get off, go find myself a resource, and there will be no subsistence or any provisions made until I get a ship. All my baggage and gear is still over in Brooklyn on the ship. Every day, I came up here to their office at nine in the morning and waited till five for orders. This is the first day and about the second time, and I'm tried of waiting already. It's no use writing me anymore on the *Costa Rica*. Just wait until I send you a new address.

Have you gotten a passport through the mail for me? I think I'm going to have to have it before I ship out again, so if you do have it, hang on to it till I tell you what to do with it.

I've seen just about everything here in New York that I want to, so the quicker they get me out of here, the better I'll like it. I went out to Coney Island just to see what it was like. Rode on the roller coaster and a few of the big rides and then left. I've ridden these subways so much I'm beginning to know them like a book. If you just miss one stop, you're liable to go twenty-five streets too far. They really make good time.

I saw *Oklahoma*, a very good performance. All the singing, acting, costumes, and players were good. Also went to a radio show at the RCA Building. Got the ticket to go at the Stage Door Canteen. Was passing by and saw the sign saying Stage Door Canteen—hadn't heard about it, so I decided to go and look around. They give you all you want to eat, a hostess comes over and talks to you while eating, and then there is a band and dancing.

Everywhere in New York is crowded with people, and they're always in a hurry. I'll be waiting and waiting here.

Love,
Frank

Letter 15
New York, New York, USA
May 18, 1945

Dearest Mother and Dad,

Still here at the cadet office waiting on a ship. There were about eight or ten that have already left this morning, so maybe it won't be so long before I get a ship.

The weather is very changeable, and it's raining cold; the next it is hot with the sun shining. We have to wear our Blues with stiff collars, and they get quite uncomfortable at times.

There are more cadets than ships, so consequently they are doubling up on some of the ships. I knew a couple of these boys that are up here at the Pass.

Several new Victorians are being launched in Baltimore, so I might end up on one of those. American-Hawaiian is getting several new C-4 ships. I was planning to get on one of those and went down to the

American-Hawaiian office to find out about them. They are due to be ready on the nineteenth, but a delay in construction will cause them to be a month late, so that deal is out.

Several boys come in every day from the Pacific all with their tales about their various experiences. Some of these boys just getting their orders this morning are being flown to Panama to catch the ship. Several are going to the Persian Gulf. Maybe I'll get one to the Persian Gulf also.

Well, till more news comes along.

Love,
Frank

Letter 16
Brooklyn, New York, USA
May 20, 1945

Dearest Mother and Dad,

I hope to be assigned a ship tomorrow, as up to now they haven't done so. I'm not doing anything much. I saw another radio show last night at Radio City, the *Ted Variety Show*.

I'm still sleeping on the ship, though I'm really not supposed to. I was detached from the ship last Wednesday, and when detached you're supposed to leave, but they don't mind if I sleep here, and it's much better than trying to find a room.

I got Ann's letter yesterday, the first letter I've gotten that has been written since I got back. I would like to go and see those people, but I have to go up to the cadet office every day from nine until five, so I don't believe I'll have time. That letter was a special-delivery airmail and still took twelve days to get here. I hope my letters do not keep that long before getting there.

Everyone must be excited about getting out of school and fluttering around. I'll write again tomorrow.

Love,
Frank

Letter 17
New York, New York, USA
May 21, 1945

Inherent Financial Acumen with the Use of the Phrase "In the Red"

Dear Ann,

Got your airmail special just twelve days after you wrote it. It was extra good to hear from you and find out about these parts. I'd like to go down and see those people, but I don't think I'll have time.

I've been to about all the places you mentioned except down Riverside Drive. You know—if I had only hit here about a month later, maybe you could come up. If I get a ship running to England or France, it'll only take about six weeks for a complete trip, so I'll be back in before very long.

It seems like eternity since the day we got in. They switch us around so much and never seem to accomplish very much by doing so. I hope today's the day I'll get a ship.

Are you planning to do the same this summer as last? That seemed like a fairly good deal for a gal like you.

You know what I've just come to the realization of? That it's easy to spend money around here. What do you think about that? I thought there was a possibility of saving a little in this cadet corps, but the poor cadets who hit New York are more likely to go "in the red."

I'm hoping I'll get a ship heading for the Pacific, but the Atlantic is so near that'll probably be my traveling waters again.

Take care, honey, little brother will write again before long.

Love and everything else,
Frank

Letter 18
New York, New York, USA
May 23, 1945

SS *Red Bank Victory Assignment*

Dearest Mother and Dad,

They assigned me a ship yesterday, and like all the rest they were assigning, it is a tanker. It was commissioned on November 11, so it's nearly new, but it doesn't look so. It's been traveling in the North Atlantic, so it's rather beat up.

We are going to leave in a couple of days, and I think the trip will be a short one.

My address is:

C/M.D. Frank B. Bradshaw U.S.M.M.C.C.
SS Red Bank Victory
c/o Postmaster

New York, New York
American Republics Corp.

There is room for four cadets in the room I'm staying in, but I'm the only cadet aboard. I don't know if there will be any more cadets before we leave. None of the officers on this ship are King Point men, and there is a marked difference.

I don't see anything about this ship up to par with the *Costa Rica*. I haven't met the captain, because a new one is coming aboard and he has not arrived yet. We are going to some place about fifty miles away from New York to load up.

I had to get all my baggage from Brooklyn to Jersey City, and I'm not exaggerating when I say it was about the hardest job I ever did.

I had the seabag, footlocker, and suitcase. All were full and heavy as lead. I had to carry it, go in subways, use taxicabs, go on ferries, and go through tunnels to get here. To top it off, after crossing the Hudson River on a ferry, I had to walk about a mile with this stuff to the ship because they wouldn't let any vehicles go to the piers.

We were supposed to go to this place down in New Jersey this morning at six, but it is now eight in the morning, and we haven't gone yet. Something broke down in the engine room.

I'll let you know more about the situation soon.

Love,
Frank

Letter 19
Atlantic Ocean
May 31, 1945

Educate
Love for Family
American Dreams

Dearest Mother and Dad,

We've been out to sea for over a week and should be over halfway to England by now. We don't know where we're going as to the parts. I will probably be on the Liverpool side of the island and close by Bristol.

My opinion of tankers is still practically the same, though they have their good points.

I'm doing some more work on this ship than the last, but it is no more than six hours a day, and I'm not doing anything too hard, so I'm not kicking about it.

At the last minute, we got two new officers aboard that are really swell. One of them is a King's Point man, the second mate; we get along fine, and he helps me out as much as he can.

I usually work on deck from eight to twelve in the morning. I'm off all evening until six o'clock, and then I go on the bridge for a couple of hours until eight. I really enjoy being on the bridge those couple of hours. I've learned much more on this trip than the last, so I'm very glad I had the change.

I've thought about this sea life and looked the old-timers over that have been out here for forty or fifty years. For six months or a year, it is fine; seeing the world is probably the most educational period of life. After that, the art of sailing and staying on the sea does not offer a very wide field for anyone with much thought or initiative.

After a year or six months, you've learned about all that I'd ever want about a ship and traveling for days on the water. Seeing nothing but water gets very monotonous and dulling on the mind.

You probably think this isn't so, but I've noticed these guys that stayed out here a long time, and it's hard to explain, but they all have some peculiar trait about them. It seems that they live because they nearly have to exist, and after so long a time, I would call it not living but existing.

At home, I never was awake all night in my bunk because of being shaken around. Out here, you have plenty of time to think out nearly every little problem that ever enters the mind. You can't imagine how tiresome this gets and how you get to feel about things at times.

I found out from other cadets in New York how hard it was for them to study at sea. It is hard to sit down and really get much done. I don't care how much you try. Reading is the only pastime; it seems to be relaxing, so I read a good bit.

I like the captain all right. I'll have to tell you more about him later. He is quite a character. He's been nice to me and never gives me a hard time. There are some guys that rejoice in doing this if they have the slightest chance.

Another thing is the crew. You practically have to get along with them to make out. The cadet is in the most awkward position on the ship. The officers are one branch, and the cadets are another branch, so we associate with them about two-thirds of the working day, eating on the bridge, talking, etc.

For the purpose of learning, it is imperative to be on deck and be with the crew some of the time. Since there are so many of them, they are the other branch of the ship. The crew usually doesn't like the officers too much. It is the cadet's job to get along with both the officers and the crew, while the officers just have to get along with the officers and the crew with the crew and the cadet with both. It's a messed-up affair.

A couple of nights ago, the blackout was terminated, and now this ocean looks like Coney Island lit up at night with all these ship lights beaming in all directions and all colors, such as red, green, etc.

We've had very nice weather for the North Atlantic, but still the fact remains it's the North Atlantic, and you couldn't expect too much.

I have a new engine-room cadet, a nice fellow who is out for the first time. I've been doctoring on him all day for several days. He complained of seasickness. I try to help him out all I can 'cause he tells me when he has to go down in the engine room he nearly dies.

I have the dreamiest sleep I've ever had in my life. All night, every night is one big dream, and boy what my mind can think up. I wouldn't put it in the books.

All the quarters on a tanker for the cadets are aft. We are over the propeller. It turns over about 90 rpm, and we can feel every one of them. At first, anyway, but now we're getting used to it. This ship hits about fifteen knots and vibrates like that machine of Daddy's all the time.

Since I've been out here on this trip, I've gotten the idea I'd like to have a ranch. Oh, for the life of a rancher. It might have been too many fictions, but I've always wanted to go down on a ranch for a while. All those wide-open spaces are what I like. That's the main thing I like about the ocean—it's so big. All around, everything is so clean and clear, and nothing in the way to obstruct or hinder it in any way.

I bought myself a whole box of Hershey's, gum, and mints. Just eat candy and chew gum till my jaws hurt.

I saw two more old whales puffing around and sending up spurts of water in continuous intervals today.

At one time, I thought I would like to take to pleasure crews around the world, but now that thought has changed.

I'll stick to an airplane when this worldwide tour takes place. It seems to me we'll all just have to fill the plane up and take the trip all together.

Since I've been on here, I've heard some of the tallest tales told in so much earnestness that it's almost pathetic.

I hold all of you in the highest esteem and love you so much.

Frank

Letter 20

Avonmouth, England
June 10, 1945

Worship

Dearest Mother and Daddy,

Today is Sunday, although I'd never know it unless the calendar said so. The atmosphere of a real Sunday is far away. Someday soon, I hope to put away for good these Sundays on the sea and revert back to the dry land with the church around the corner. The last time I went to church was in Baltimore. I looked down at my watch; it read eleven in the morning—this is what made me think of all of this.

It must be nice and warm there in Memphis by now. We're heading for a hot climate; now, however, we're on a parallel with Salvador, so the weather is not too warm.

We arrived in Avonmouth, a port only four miles from Bristol, on June 4 at three o'clock in the morning. Immediately they began unloading.

The next morning, which was still the fourth, the other cadet and myself decided to dress and take a trip to London, just to see it and also get the ride through the country. Since we were up all night getting docked, we didn't get up till about ten thirty. We dressed, walked about a mile to the gate of the shipyard, and then took a taxi to the bus, which was headed for Bristol.

We rode along the Avon River to Bristol. The scenery was beautiful, everything green, and the houses being all built of stone, which was nice and clean. When we got in Bristol, we went to the railroad station and bought a round-trip ticket for a pound ($4.02). The dinner we ate at the hotel in Bristol wasn't any good.

At two thirty in the afternoon, we left for London on a very strange-looking train. For every pair of seats, there was a door on each side of the coach to get out. The train stopped at various places about every hour, where refreshments could be bought.

A little after six o'clock, we arrived in London. From the train station, we went on an underground train to Piccadilly Circus, the Times Square of London. We went to the Red Cross and ate supper, and then we went on a little tour around the city. We went to the House of Parliament, House of Commons, Westminster Abbey, Buckingham Palace, Westminster Bridge, Big Ben, Scotland Yard, Churchill's house, several of the big parks. Then we went back to Piccadilly Circus and fooled around for a couple of hours. We took the train out of Paddington Station.

After a long ride then a long walk, we got back to the ship about seven o'clock the next morning. The last few gallons of gasoline were being pumped out as we came aboard. After securing all the tankers and testing the bridge equipment, we were towed by tugs through the docks—and then were on our way. The ship was only in England for about twenty-six hours, and we were ashore about twenty-three.

The monotony of the sea is what I don't like about tankers. Since I called you all on the twenty-third, I've only been on land for that short time in England. And still have about ten days to go before seeing it again.

I sent a cablegram in Bristol. Did you ever get it? The last time I had any mail was on May 12. I don't know what these postmasters do with it.

Every day except for one we've had rough weather. The wind always is blowing hard, and it is misty, foggy, and damp all the time. Another thing—did you ever get those war bonds that I sent in the letter?

All my clothes are as dirty as the dirt itself. I'm hoping to get them cleaned and washed down there with some soap and water.

Our food has been fine on this ship. Better than the food on the *Costa Rica*.

Letter 21
Atlantic Ocean
June 15, 1945

Now I can't say the weather is cold. Eggs can be fried on the deck. We're about four hundred miles off the coast of Florida. Supposed to reach Galveston on the nineteenth—if the orders are not changed again. We've had hot, sunny weather the last couple of days. I've acquired a nice reddish tan.

We paused a few miles north of Bermuda Island last night, though I was not up to see it.

All week, the junior third mate and myself have been checking the lifeboat equipment, overhauling it, etc.

I'd like to get Buford's, Larry's, Richard's, and Jacob's address if you could dig them up.

We've had fine sleeping for the last week. We have two fans in our room and three ports so the weather can get very hot and still we'll sleep.

I only got a few coins from England as a souvenir.

Letter 22
Galveston, Texas, USA
June 19, 1945

Educate

Yes, we're lying at anchor in the lazy, hazy harbor of Galveston, Texas. The very sight of this land drives the thousand miles of loneliness, which usually raises such havoc with the mind, far into the background—or, may I say, not away, but to be forgotten for a while.

The ever-changing flux of going to sea and—every time, so far, in my case—going to a different port and seeing different sights always gives a thrill and a little surprise to what you'll see.

We passed two and one-half miles off the shore of Palm Beach and likewise as close all the distance down the coast of Florida and also the Keys. The sailing for the last seven days has been serene with blue-sky water and the temperature just a small above what we class as very pleasant weather.

Much, much controversy is already taking place about the next voyage of the SS *Red Bank Victory*, which evidently I will be on. To the Pacific is the ever-sounding cry in the air, though no confirmation has been made of any reports; consequently, we could be heading for almost anyplace. We're sure the ship is headed for dry dock for at least five days.

My nautical studious capacity is undoubtedly very small. My mathematics book has been completed and forgotten, is still lingering in the rafters with blank pages.

When we get ashore and get around, I'll be able to give you more of a description about this land of tiptoe shoes.

All my love,
Frank

Letter 23
Texas City, Texas, USA
June 27, 1945

Worship
Love for Family

Dearest Mother and Dad,

We stayed in Houston until Sunday night having a fine, super-duper time. We slept at the USO Saturday night, got up, went to church Sunday morning.

The other cadet went to a Catholic church and I to the Presbyterian church, so we were to meet back in front of the USO. A car came by just as we got there; also several soldiers were standing there, and they asked us if we would like to go swimming. Everyone was willing, so the whole bunch piled into the care (fourteen in all), and we rode what seemed like miles and miles out into the country. We ended up at a beauty of a country club, had dinner, went swimming, played tennis.

There were plenty of nice girls around, so we went back into Houston and had a date that night. We had a fine time.

Monday, we left dry dock and proceeded out into Galveston Bay to wait for orders. This morning, we were directed to go to Texas City, just about an hour's run from Galveston. Now we are restricted to the ship, and I don't know when, if at all, the restriction will be lifted.

The surprise, as to the direction we're headed in, is still in the air. Monday, before leaving dry dock, I went to the office with the captain. I heard them tell him they had no idea in the world as to where the ship was heading.

It's hot as fire here, and to make it worse, we have gotten a rotten cook aboard this time.

My laundry is still in Galveston, so somehow or other, I've got to get it tonight.

I enjoyed talking with all of you immensely last Saturday. Everyone sounded natural as could be, and I could hear much plainer than usual.

We possibly may be here four or five days yet and even may go to some other ports for a deck cargo. I'll let you know when something happens.

Frank

Letter 24
Caribbean Sea
July 1, 1945

Another Sunday at Sea
Love for Family
Love for Country

Dearest Mother and Dad,

In the sky-blue water of the Caribbean Sea, we are sweating it out. The impact of another Sunday at sea—which is practically over, as the time is nine o'clock at night—is driving more loneliness in our souls. Speculation of the future for the next few days provides wishful thoughts. We are keeping to get ashore in Panama. This will be the last chunk of solid soil that'll be on view for about a month.

Today we passed through the straits of Yucatan and were a couple of miles off the "Land of Rum and Coca-Cola," or what is so commonly called the Isle of Cuba. We would be making much better time, but we're on watch to avoid submarines.

From summertime, oh sweet summertime, to wintertime, dull, old wintertime, we shall go.

The calls were more than a pleasure and a shining morale builder to me; they make me feel the nearness of home. Though the last was on the sympathetic side, which I dislike, I enjoyed the sound of your voices and the things you do for me. Any of the various times that I might have a chance to cable or communicate in any, any form, I'll do so.

My mind seems to be oblivious of all news tonight; the saying goes, though, that sometimes no news is the best news.

Letter 25
Isthmus of Panama
July 3, 1945

Hope the War Ends Soon

Nearing the isthmus, not being too many hours away with a rough sea, makes us want to get there even more.

I wish I could say truthfully that I was looking forward to going back to King's Point. All I can say—the sooner the war is over, the better it will suit me. Comparatively speaking with a bunch of the other boys, I have only been out a short time—enough, though, to have me thoroughly fed up.

Enough of that sort of rambling talk. The sound of those rich, red strawberries and those chickens make my mouth water every time I think of them. The greatest one item I miss is milk. We have canned milk for coffee, and that's the limit.

We're here. Don't know how long. Probably only a very short time. The weather is cool enough here.

For the last day or so, the wind and sea have been choppy.

Will write again soon.

Love,
Frank

Letter 26
South Pacific
August 11, 1945

Japan Surrenders
Educate
Formerly in Adelaide, Australia
Letters from July 3 to August 11 were either lost or censored.

Dear Mother and Daddy,

We've heard the good news today about Tokyo considering surrender. We heard it direct from Tokyo. Wouldn't that be fine? Wonder how long the draft would last after they do surrender. I've pretty much made up my mind not to go back to King's Point. It's now a three-year course, and I wouldn't want to fool around with it that long. I'd rather start in on some college work. If I could start that soon, I wouldn't be much behind my regular peacetime schedule.

I'm not sure where I'll want to go to college as yet.

Either to the University of Tennessee or some school toward the west would be my guess now. I don't know if being in the MM will compensate for any money for education after getting out.

We were last in Adelaide, South Australia. It is about the size of Memphis. We were here for two days, giving plenty of time to go ashore as much as we wanted to.

I don't think it will be very long before we head back for the States. Seems like now we are to make one short shuttle run and then head back.

Letter 27
Perth, Australia
August 13, 1945

World War II Is Over

In port again. Perth and Fremantle, West Australia. Heard the unconfirmed news today that the war is over. You can't imagine how good that makes me feel. I can't even start to realize that it is over.

I know that I won't go back to King's Point for two years in peacetime. Probably in two or three months, the draft will stop for all boys over eighteen. By that time, I'll be nineteen and all set to get out. Let me know what Billy and Jasper are going to do about the cadet corps.

We haven't been ashore here yet. We are going to shift positions in a couple of hours, and then we'll have a chance to go ashore. We might have our ship fumigated here at the port. If so, we will be here for a few days.

This is our fourth post in Australia. Hobart, Melbourne, Adelaide, Fremantle, and Perth. Fremantle and Perth are only a few miles apart.

When I get off this trip and have a leave at home, I would like to make one more trip to South America on a freighter. I've always wanted to go down there, and this is as good of a chance as any.

I'll probably be owing the company money at the end of this trip. I've made more draws than I can count, spending more money around here than I'm making.

As usual, when we hit a British port, it is raining. All day long, it rains without a single letup.

I don't know if we'll be heading back for the States. If not now, it'll be in the near future.

I just got through reading a good book on agriculture. A new slant on how to farm seemed like it was practical.

We're moving now.

Love,
Frank

Letter 28
Manila, Philippine Islands
November 2, 1945

Formerly in Abadan, Iran, and Singapore
United States Supplying Iran and Singapore with Oil after World War II
Without External Threat, the Probability of Internal Disorder, Confusion,
and Chaos Increases
Letters from August 13 to November 2 were either lost or censored.

Dear Mother and Dad,

Well, folks, we've finally hit port again. Yes, sir, we hit these ports, but we're out of them nearly by the time we get in. After leaving Abadan, we headed for Singapore. It took us eleven days to get to Singapore, where we thought we were going to discharge. After pondering around here with the naval authorities for a couple of days, they sent us here to Manila. We thought surely we would discharge here, but since we've gotten here, they want us to go somewhere else to unload. Gosh! I hope they make up their minds before long. We're practically sure to be heading back after this cargo has gotten to be a permanent possession of the ship. In the harbor are quite a few captured Japanese warships. I never have seen so many ships in all my life: sunk ones, captured ones, freighters, tankers, US Navy, and transports and subs. I wonder if Fred ever was here.

Singapore was in a wild tumult, skyrocket prices, no stability in any form. Half-naked soldiers running around and no one doing much of anything.

Most of the sea trip we had good weather, though for a couple of days it was rather on the rough side. In Singapore I had a fuss with the captain. He was making false accusations against me, so I called his bluff. Everything is okay now.

If we come into Panama and this ship is coming back out here, I'm going to get off there and get home some way or another. If we follow the schedule as we're supposed to now, we'll be in by Christmas. The last letter I got was written in the middle of August.

All my love,
Frank

Letter 29
Los Angeles, California, USA
December 1945

The Biltmore Hotel

Dear Mother and Dad,

I've been moving around so much with small petty matters to attend to this is my first chance to drop a line.

In San Pedro with the ship out in the harbor for the first four days, then finally pulling into the docks, and then having a delayed payoff, prolonged my stay here in California by at least a week.

After getting our baggage shipped and obtaining our seaman's papers, which took an extra two days, the other cadet and myself went to San Francisco. Before we left here the first time, we managed to see part of Hollywood and its surroundings.

Traveled by train to Frisco, getting there Sunday morning. Got a room, saw the town, and piddled around till Monday. Wednesday at one o'clock, we were completely through with the cadet corps. In the office in Frisco, they were very cordial. We had to turn the clothes in at San Mateo, where they tried to give us a hard time, acting as 99 percent of the cadet officers do. They were arrogant, trying to make you subjugated until the last minute; all they accomplished was to make a heel out of themselves.

Thursday we got Richard's seaman's paper and then caught the plane that night. We were going to Tucson, but we couldn't get reservations on the plane, train, or bus.

Richard called Mr. Vaughn; he's going to drive out and pick us up. He'll be here sometime tonight. We'll leave for Tucson Saturday morning and get there late Saturday night (six hundred miles).

The Vaughns are coming to Memphis for Christmas, so I'll ride with them. I don't know yet when we'll leave Tucson.

I've had a wonderful time since we landed on the West Coast. After a trip, it's really good to relax and enjoy ashore. We haven't tried to be frugal or cut many corners; consequently, I've found that this West Coast will devour money at an amazing rate.

The trip through the country is bound to be interesting and enjoyable. I'm glad it will be by auto.

With my love,
Frank

Letter 30
Galveston, Texas, USA
February 9, 1946

Dear Mother and Dad,

Everything has been running smooth for the last couple of days. Still cleaning tanks, though it's easy because we don't work half the time. We get off today at twelve o'clock and don't have to come back until Monday morning. Berlin has gone to Houston, so when I get off today at twelve, Richard and I are going to Houston and then coming back tonight with Berlin's aunt. She is going to drive us back down.

Haven't had any luck getting either of them on the ship. One guy was fired this morning, so this may possibly give an opening to Berlin because he held the same rating as Berlin holds.

I'm finishing this letter, riding in on a launch. It's raining, and the wind is blowing fairly hard. Two ships bumped into each other just a few hundred yards from where we're anchored; no one was hurt.

Well, I'll let you hear soon, especially if anything else develops.

Love,
Frank

Letter 31
Le Havre, France
March 7, 1946

War-Damage Assessment
Love of Family
Letters from February 9 to March 7 were either lost or censored.

Dear Mother and Dad,

We arrived today about four in the afternoon and were tied up at the docks around six in the evening. The trip over was much as anticipated: quite a bit of rough weather and also cold. It was snowing when we got here, and the weather is below freezing.

Several of the guys got seasick coming over.

From what I can see of Le Havre, it is about half-demolished. We didn't get ashore until after dark. I haven't seen much. We are coming back tomorrow morning.

Half of our cargo will be discharged here, and then we're going up the Seine River halfway to Paris to discharge the other half. Probably be here about a week.

I hope my draft board situation is straightened out by the time I get back. I'll call home before I sign off the ship. The way I feel now, I would like to take my fifteen-day leave when I get back. We'll go back to Texas.

I miss all of you and can't get back soon enough.

Love,
Frank

Letter 32
Atlantic Ocean
March 21, 1946

Aruba Oil to Brazil
War-Damage Assessment
High Morale—Good Work with Other Sailors
Formerly in Azores

Dear Mother and Dad,

Today, for the first time since we left France, the weather is decent.

It was a surprise to all of us that the ship was diverted to Aruba. This is a small island just off the coast of Venezuela. We picked up gasoline here and are going to take it to Santos, Brazil. Wasn't that a coincidence? Planning to go to South America all the time and getting there in a roundabout way. We will drive in Aruba on the twenty-third, leave on the twenty-fifth. It will take us eleven or twelve days to get to Santos if good weather prevails.

France was a nice country to see; Le Havre and Rouen, we tore up badly. The Azores are a beautiful little clump of islands.

I wondered if you got my radiogram. I sent it from the ship.

I have a good mate and my watch, and the days seem to be clicking off fairly fast now that I'm used to it. Several boys are my age, so we have a pretty good time playing around. Will write again soon.

Love,
Frank

Letter 33
San Nicholas, Aruba
March 26, 1946

Aruba Equals Oil
Ship Chartered by the Rockefeller's Oil Company

Dear Mother and Dad,

We're still in Aruba, got in early on the morning of the twenty-third, and half of our cargo to Brazil was kerosene, which we were all loaded and ready to get yesterday. A cable came from Brazil that they didn't want any kerosene, so now we are pumping all of it out and filling up with gas. The ship is now chartered by Standard Oil, the Rockefellers' oil company. We don't know what our orders from Santos will be.

This is a pretty little island, about twenty miles long and about like on the coast in the summertime.

If you ever want to get in touch with me in a hurry, send a

radiogram through the Western Union with my address on it. Then they will wire it out here to the ship.

This should be called the Island of Standard Oil; they monopolize all the business, and everything is centered around the refinery and quite a place. It's all the difference in the world where the war has been and where it hasn't. We're leaving in the morning. I write from Santos.

Love,
Frank

Letter 34
Willemstad, Curacao
April 21, 1946

Formerly in the Mediterranean and Persian Gulf
United States Supplying Mediterranean and Persian Gulf Countries
with Oil
Letters from March 26 to April 21 were either lost or censored.

Dear Mother and Dad,

Well, we are loading again, today; you know what this means—we're going someplace else. This time it's England. The orders were changed, thus we ended up here in Curacao. Curacao is an island about seventy-five miles east of Aruba. It's one of the Netherlands West Indies, and most of the people are Dutchmen and natives.

If they send us back from England, everything will be perfect. I'll have a month leave providing the draft is still on; if it's not, the situation will be better still. We should be back around the fifteenth of May. I only hope they will not send us through the Mediterranean and to the Persian Gulf again.

A merchant marine strike is supposed to come off in about three weeks. If this ship gets back to the States, they won't be able to get a crew. Consequently, she will have to be tied up. I doubt if the company will let this happen if they can possibly help it.

Coming back from Santos, naturally the chief engineer thought we were going to the States, so he sped her up. We were doing twenty-five miles per hour. We went 4,800 miles in eight days—that's good traveling for any merchant ship. We should make to England in ten or twelve days, depending largely on current and weather conditions.

There's very little to do here in Curacao. A couple of good movies and nothing more.

They told us in our orders that we were going to the United Kingdom. This probably means England, Scotland, or Ireland, but still the United Kingdom extends all over the world, so maybe we'll end up in Australia or South Africa.

There are a couple of good guys on the ship, and the mate on my watch is okay, so I get along pretty well with my work. My main job is steering, also stand an hour of lookout at night. I've bought her in and taken her out of every port.

I got my first mail, five letters. I'll let you know more news later.

Love,
Frank

Letter 35
Atlantic Ocean
April 22, 1946

Drunk in Every Port
Food Is Getting Worse
Illicit Sex on the High Seas
Disorder, Confusion, and Chaos Erupt When War Is Over

Dear Mother and Dad,

Left Curacao at twelve o'clock this noon. As usual, it was my luck to take her out again. Two days were long enough in such a place. I've seen worse, but still this was nothing to brag about.

We lost two men in Curacao, one with an ulcerated stomach and one with ulcers on his legs. Another guy here has a terrible case of varicose veins. The doctor told him to drink, but this was the worst thing for it—every port we've hit, this guy has been drunk the whole time. This evening, one of those veins was bad, so now they're having a time trying to patch him up.

As I've probably said before, the food is getting worse every day, and now to the point where it's terrible. I've lost at least ten pounds. I guess I'll lose some more.

The captain is about the craziest loon I've ever seen. He's radical and jumps up and down and beats his head when we get in a tight spot. On the trip from Galveston to France and from France to Aruba, he had a woman hid up in his room.

(There were cutouts here—apparently censored.)

I knew something was curious because every day when I'd take the noon report to him from the bridge, he would have his room and office locked and barred.

(There were cutouts here—apparently censored.)

Well, one day, the lights shorted out, and the electrician had to go in there. That's when we were sure.

(There were cutouts here—apparently censored.)

This captain was born in Belgium. The coast guard caught him in Aruba, and they took the woman off. I was surprised I did not hear that the captain was either reprimanded or brought up on charges.

The sea is calm tonight, and the temperature is about eighty-five. Don't know yet where we're going in England.

Letter 36
Atlantic Ocean
April 27, 1946

South Carolina Coast

Out five days now, this being the first day the weather is beginning to roughen up a bit. Also it is getting chilly. We're off the South Carolina coast about a thousand miles out. The days are passing so slow. Seems like we'll never get there.

This goofy captain is putting a tarpaulin over the wheel on the flying bridge. We're going to have to stand our wheel watch up there. In the hot weather down in the tropics, we stayed in the wheelhouse. Now the weather is getting bad, we're going on the outside to steer.

Heading in the vicinity of the English Channel; haven't gotten our port of destination yet. Probably will be in the London area. I wish we would go to Ireland.

Have been listening over shortwave about the draft. What I've heard, they sound like they can't make up their minds. Maybe it will expire the fifteenth. There's hope, anyway.

Frank

Letter 37
North Atlantic
May 3, 1946

Trouble with the Captain of the Ship
Food Shortage and Petition
Disorder

One day out of England; supposed to dock sometime tomorrow evening. As yet, we don't know where we're going. They got the orders, but the captain won't tell us. This is one more on the list of agitations due to him. All these little things like this, he'll do just for spite.

We're out of food nearly completely and have been out the whole trip, so we got up a petition to do the captain to obtain some more food in England. This should bear some weight because four copies are being made and are going to be sent to the right places in the States. If the captain doesn't get some more food, he'll probably be in trouble when he gets back to the States. It's caused some of the guys to get sick enough so they couldn't stand their watch. I've been feeling okay, eating a lot of cereal and canned milk.

If the captain will consent, I'm going to get him to pay me off here in England, and then I can catch a plane home and be there in no time. I'm afraid this ship is going to the Persian Gulf.

We're out of it now, but for the last five days, we have been on the outskirts of a cyclone. The wind was so strong we couldn't hardly get to the bridge, and the waves were coming over the whole ship.

Frank

Letter 38
Avonmouth, England
May 4, 1946

Confusion

We got in this afternoon about three o'clock, and guess where? It's the same place I went when on the SS *Red Bank Victory*. We're docked in Avonmouth, which is about five miles from Bristol.

There's been a lot of trouble with the steward's department. The crew had a special meeting today, and if possible, we are going to get some more cooks and a new steward.

Also the captain is going to hospital. He's got some kind of sores in his mouth. With all this confusion, we're liable to be here a few days.

We haven't gotten any orders where to go from here. The general opinion is that we're heading back for the States, but you know what opinions mean. We had definite orders from France and also from Santos, and still they were changed both times.

England is still the same, cold and misty.

The bad news has just come; we're going back to Aruba. Don't know where from there. I'm trying to get off. More news later.

Love,
Frank

Letter 39
Atlantic Ocean
May 7, 1946

High Seas Cheating and Fraud
Low Morale and High Chaos
No Bombs, No Gratitude

Dear Mother and Dad,

Left Avonmouth last night at nine o'clock heading back for Aruba. Now isn't that another stroke of luck. We thought for sure we were going back home.

We got as many supporters as possible; that petition did the job. The captain fretted and made threats that he would make us pay for signing, but this is a lot of hot air because there's nothing he can do legally.

We have proof that this captain is doing underhanded work, trying to make money on the government and swindling the men aboard. The crew is going as a group when we get to Aruba to take the captain off the ship. When I get home, I'll tell you what we have on him. The ship stays in chaos nearly all the time.

We should make it to Aruba on the seventeenth at the rate we're now sailing, making eighteen knots, due to a strong following sea, and also we are light.

Spent one day in Bristol and one in Avonmouth. Bristol is a nice place: shows and some nice landscape and historic places. Only trouble was that the wind was blowing hard, and it was cold as the devil. England isn't starving to death, but still, they are desperately short of foodstuffs and all other commodities. These people have been through quite a bit, evidence shows, but the thing I don't like is they think they won the war by themselves. They take it for granted that America should supply them, and then they don't pay for it or express any gratitude. I was talking to one who said why shouldn't America supply them if we have plenty and they don't. Another thing they figure is we really haven't been in the war because they were bombed and we weren't.

Frank

Letter 40
Atlantic Ocean
May 12, 1946

Hope of Last Trip

Opposite Memphis today, only three thousand miles to the east. Should be in Aruba the sixteenth since we're still making exceptionally good time.

We got some news today. Guess what? Going back across the Atlantic when leaving Aruba. This makes three times across and one trip to South America. This trip is getting too long. Besides, this next trip is going to be a bit longer. First we're going to Hamburg, Germany, to discharge half of the cargo. We haven't found it on the map, but it is in Denmark or East Prussia. They told us that it was in a Russian zone, so in all probability, it will be East Prussia. From there, it is the same old story. Supposedly we're coming back. I hope so, anyway. By rough calculations this should put us back around the fifteenth of June.

I heard about the draft being extended to July 1. If it will stop there, everything will be okay. A day out of Aruba. Nothing much else has happened. We have a hard time sleeping. The weather is so hot. Everyone hopes this is the last trip.

We'll enjoy it that much more when getting there.

Love,
Frank

Letter 41
Aruba
May 18, 1946

Love for Family
Cotton Business and Fishing
Get Sick and Get Off
Jump Ship and Go to Jail

Dear Mother and Dad,

I got about a dozen letters today—feel better than any time since we left. Actually getting mail is by far the greatest pleasure we have. The last letter was written on the ninth. You had received my letter from England. It was good to hear the news how everyone is getting along and about all the occurrences. I like to hear about the cotton business and Daddy's fishing trips.

Peace sounds like it's extra important. The cotton carnival, getting city water, graduation, etc. I would like to be there.

You know about the draft. Well, until July 1 doesn't make any difference now. Our first stop next trip will be Rotterdam, Holland. We're supposed to go to two or three places. Nobody knows exactly where as yet.

You ask about my weight. I haven't weighed since I've been here. When I get through writing, I'm going up town, San Nicholas, and weigh. We got some food in stores in England, but no fruit—haven't had any fruit aboard since Brazil.

We arrived here the sixteenth and haven't been able to get a berth until this morning. Since the sea was rough in our anchorage here in Aruba, one of our anchors is broken. We went down on the coast of Venezuela in a little bay and anchored. It's only a two-hour run from here. The wind is blowing the fumes from the refinery all over the ship. Boy, how it stinks.

They have a nice beach and some shows over in the Dutch settlement. We're going over there this afternoon.

Most of my clothes are worn out or in sad condition. I buy what I need out of the slop chest, such as khaki pants, shirts, etc. Only the guys that are real sick can get off, so I haven't got a chance. Six or eight are getting off. If you jump the ship here, they put you in jail, so I guess I'm on here for another trip.

I got to bring her in again this morning. Nothing to it anymore.

I'll drop you another line before we leave.

Love,
Frank

Letter 42
Hamburg, Germany
June 3, 1946

Formerly in Rotterdam, Holland
The Black Market

Dear Mother and Dad,

I wrote Ann a letter in Rotterdam and meant to get off at least two to the family, but since we stayed there just for one day, I didn't have much time. Rotterdam is about twenty miles up the river from the sea, so we saw a little bit of Holland going up, and then we went ashore in Rotterdam. The land is very flat, and they still have their windmills. These windmills are big twice as big as any other I've seen. The Dutch are very clean people, and Rotterdam was likewise. The biggest business in Rotterdam is the black market. They deal in everything and are everyplace. Nearly all of these people can speak English. Most of these people speak four languages.

I'm on watch now, two in the morning.

Hamburg is in the English occupational zone, and Gdansk, Poland, is in the Russian zone, though it might be governed by the Poles.

If you noticed on the map, these places are on high northerly latitudes. Since the sea has a northerly declination of about twenty degrees, we have only four hours of darkness per day. The rest of the time, she's light, something like the midnight summer of the Eskimos.

The month of June is supposed to be the summertime. You would never know it by the weather. It's cold as a Memphis winter day, and the wind usually blows about twenty to forty miles per hour out here in the North Sea.

I'm not getting my hopes up, but so far, our orders read to return to Galveston when discharged. If they are not changed, we should make it in about June 20.

Frank

Letter 43
Kiel Canal, Germany
June 5, 1946

War-Damage Assessment
Cold-Blooded Slaughter in Odessa, Ukraine

Just left Hamburg, and what a port. Different from all the rest. For American cigarettes, you could get anything or practically any amount of money. One thousand marks for a carton, the exchange value before the war was four marks to a dollar. Now it is ten marks to a dollar. This would be one hundred dollars per carton. I didn't think the money would be any good, so I just traded around and got a couple of souvenirs. Now since we left, I found out that it is good in Poland.

We're going through a canal now that is a hundred miles long, cutting off the whole peninsula of Denmark. This saves at least a day and a half run. The shore people put quartermasters on to steer, so all I have to do is to sit back and take it easy. This canal is about 250 feet wide. That's not much for a ship making turns, etc. We get out of the canal at seven tonight, and then it's three hundred miles across the Baltic Sea to Danzig.

You would be surprised at how beautiful a country Germany is. They have some magnificent buildings and structural works. That is, what is left.

Hamburg was hit the hardest of any city I've seen. In some places, there is not so much as a wall standing for miles. We rode four miles in a British Army car through a section of town that was nothing but piles of bricks. For these four miles, everything was demolished. They rode us over the town to see the sights. The talk in the States of this country starving is just politics and a scheme for some big business to make a big profit. The only thing that they are really short on is sugar and coffee. All along the banks goes the Elbe River, and along this canal, we have seen thousands of cattle and crops in the field. No one is dying of starvation or even going hungry. There're just as many people that are dying in the States as over here.

Naturally, these guys think they are going to rise to power again. In the course of a few years, they will rise again if not checked. They are smart in science and stupid in psychology. In this canal, we've passed under several magnificent bridges, four or five miles long and very high. These are the bridges of the superhighways here in Germany built for military purposes.

Now we're through the canal and have come to anchor just outside, waiting for daybreak.

This is the Kiel Canal.

Germany is the most interesting and has more sights than any other country. Much of the land, trees, birds, dogs, etc., are like those in the States. They have big fine-looking horses, all sleek and fat, looking like show horses.

Heard of a story of cold-blooded slaughter in Odessa, Ukraine.

German prisoners of war were unloading fifty- and hundred-pound bags of sugar when one fell to the ground between handoffs and broke open at the seams. They clustered around the sugar and began to eat because they were starving. The very large and well-fed female guards with rags on their heads as bandanas and with machine guns at the ready did not like the sight of Germans eating food destined for Ukrainian people. The guards yelled "Nyet!" but when the prisoners continued to eat, the guards opened fired on the defenseless German POWs and mowed them down with a shower of bullets. About a half-dozen POWs were killed. Human blood, hair, and bits of guts were splattered about three feet from the slain victims. The guards made the prisoners clean the blood and other human remains from the dock to bury their dead. I don't think this will ever happen again. Will write again soon.

Love,
Frank

Postcard
Hamburg, Germany
August 8, 1973

Big, Rebuilt City
The Kiel Canal

Postcard text from Frank to his "Dearest Mother" when Frank visited Hamburg, Germany on August 8, 1973

Dear Mom,

We are in Hamburg Germany.
    Big, rebuilt city since the war.
    I was here then.
    All just fine.
    Having a good time.
    Seeing much.

The Kiel Canal was some sight.

See you before long.

Love,

Frank

Letter 44
Galveston, Texas, USA
August 9, 1946

Morale High—Good Crew

Dear Mother and Dad,

We're getting ready to go to town, so I thought I'd drop you all a line. Richard is still getting ready. He called his people last night after I called.

As I told you on the phone, the SS *Midway Hills Victory* is still in dry dock. Since practically the whole engine is out of the ship for repairs, there's no telling when she will sail, probably in about ten days. This is really what you call a ship. It is like a luxury liner compared to the SS *Quaker Hill Victory*. Good crew, food, and accommodations—of course, this is just three days on here, but I believe this will be a pleasant trip. If we make the Italy run and back to the States (I hope), it should put us in around October 1 or a little before. Have to go catch the ferry.

Love,
Frank

Letter 45
Galveston, Texas, USA
September 3, 1946

Keep a Low Profile
Ready to Be Discharged
Feeling Fine

Dear Mother and Dad,

Guess you're surprised where this letter is coming from. It's true. We're still here in Galveston on the SS *Midway Hills Victory*. You remember when she was supposed to sail? Well, the engine broke down that day, and since then, we've had several sailing dates, but every time the engine breaks down, so now they've decided to put in a new turbine. We should be here for two more weeks.

I don't want anyone but you all to know that I am still in Galveston. I'm not telling anyone, so be sure and not let it slip out to anyone. It is possible that it wouldn't make any difference, but until I get my discharge, I'd rather stay in oblivion to everyone. I'm getting regular sea time since we're signed on the articles. If I get off, it would be a few days until I could catch another ship. Since this is rather a critical period with less than a month to go, I think it best just to stay on here until October 1.

We went to Houston last weekend—saw a few shows and piddled around. Galveston is getting more monotonous and tiresome every day. Sure would like to get out of here.

Richard got a notice from his draft board about delinquency in shipping. His mother wrote some kind of letter to them that will probably fix it up.

Let me know if you hear anything from mine. My address is the same.

Feeling fine—hope all of you are the same. Also impressing on you again: no one is to know I'm still here.

Love,
Frank

I'm keeping in communication with everyone else.

Conclusion

Part I

One of my dreams is for the scientific community to continue to see God in their theories, formulas, and experiments. As such, what did I learn from my father's forty-five letters and subsequent exposure to his thoughts and conversations on the topics of worshiping God, serving, and seeking a college education? I learned to think in orders of magnitude from the smallest to the most massive structures while using numbers and calculations to make sense of the world around me.

A leap of science through faith was for me to study Proverbs in the morning and to pray so that I could better understand the universe, thereby granting me knowledge and instruction. As the ancient Greeks studied and prayed, I was able to make a similar observation, accounting for an original and significant contribution. Democritus was known for the formulation of an atomic theory of the universe because he could see atoms, but he could not measure or test them without the necessary instruments.

Similarly, I have seen the Wobble Toward Sagittarius A (WTS), which occurs when an object wobbles into place as the base of the object is pointing toward Sagittarius A. All structures wobble with a specific frequency inclination into their current locations, similar to the visual observation of a Weeble.

Sir Roger Penrose calculated that it takes a trillionth of a trillionth of a second for a human body to wobble into its present location, whereas a smaller object such as a particle of dust or possibly a flame of a candle will take approximately a second. This frequency inclination helps link relativity to quantum, matter to energy, and particle to wave, thereby possibly introducing CERN's Large Hadron Collider, which recently discovered the God particle, to discover a graviton, the key messenger between parallel universes to support the reconciliation of the relativity and quantum.

The point of this conclusion is for the scientific community to continue to see God in everyone and in everything, every day.

Conclusion
Part II

Another one of my dreams is for the general public to see God around them, supporting them and loving them. Ultimately, it is your responsibility to discover the best way to see, hear, and link to God—every day and several times a day. Study and prayer are always a good place to start. In order to stimulate this convention, I am submitting a suggestion from my research.

From Peter Higgs's *Nobel Prize in Physics* for the discovery of the God particle to Sir Roger Penrose's *The Emperor's New Mind* with quantum mechanics in our consciousness, our prayers will benefit humanity by enabling Brian Greene's *Elegant Universe*, parallel universes of peace.

Prayers originate from the oldest religion, and they will always be part of the integral fabric of our civilization. Prayers are also embedded in our souls and beings; this aspect of human nature typically requires a special time and place. The following *Vowel Pax* prayer method enables anyone at anytime to pray when his or her language is either written or spoken. The proverb for this prayer is embedded in all languages in the phonetic vowels of *a* (alpha) and *o* (omega). Perhaps you should consider that every time you see or hear the vowels *a* and *o*, you are seeing the fingerprints of God and hearing the voice of God while accepting His calling card to pray. Such a prayer can take as little as fifteen seconds, anytime and anywhere.

Step 1: Identify the *a*-alpha (aaahhh) or the *o*-omega (ooohhh) vowels in your native language. You can see these vowels in print, hear them when spoken, or identify them through any type of communication medium. This step should take you about three seconds.

Step 2: Take three breaths in three seconds while praying for help and care for your family.

Step 3: Take three breaths in three seconds while praying for help and care for your friends.

Step 4: Take three breaths in three seconds while praying for help and care for your neighbors.

Step 5: Take three breaths in three seconds while praying for help and care for the sick, needy, and poor.

The result of these prayers is peace. By thinking of helping and caring for others, your gratitude for what you have increases, and peace increases on every level and parallel.

The point of this conclusion is for the general public to see God in everyone and in everything, every day.

Conclusion
Part III

Turn to the front cover of this book. If you read the cursive manuscript closely, you will be able to discern:

> Today is Sunday, although I'd never know it unless the calendar said so. The atmosphere of a real Sunday is far away. Someday soon, I hope to put away for good these Sundays on the sea and revert back to the dry land with the church around the corner. The last time I went to church was in Baltimore. I looked down at my watch; it read eleven in the morning—this is what made me think of all of this.

Throughout my father's life, showing devotion to God played a major role in his everyday thoughts and activities. Extending his devotion beyond his love for God and for his family, he served as a sailor for more than two years, delivering sustenance to those in need from the ravages of war. After this emotionally taxing period in his life, he returned home, attended college, and showed an acute interest in mathematics. Worship, service, and education acted as key components of my father's fulfillment of his American dream.

It is my turn to fulfill my American dream through worship, service, and education. I cannot precisely emulate the honor with which my father lived his life, but I can use it as a road map for my own. I hope that reading *Forty-Five* will encourage and motivate you to take steps toward achieving your own American dream.

Worship: Love God (Mark 12:30)
Serve: Love your neighbor (Mark 12:31)
Educate: Love yourself (Mark 12:31)

Afterword

As noted in Letter 19, which my father wrote in 1945 when he was nineteen, one of his American dreams was to own a ranch one day. My father fulfilled this dream forty-five years later when he purchased a three-thousand-acre ranch in Georgia in 1990. My father fulfilled his American dream through worship, service, and education.

Appendix

<u>FRANK BERT BRADSHAW</u>

To you who answered the call of your country and served in its Merchant Marine to bring about the total defeat of the enemy, I extend the heartfelt thanks of the Nation. You undertook a most severe task—one which called for courage and fortitude. Because you demonstrated the resourcefulness and calm judgment necessary to carry out that task, we now look to you for leadership and example in further serving our country in peace.

Harry Truman

THE WHITE HOUSE

(1) President Harry Truman's thank-you to Frank Bert Bradshaw for his service in the US Merchant Marine Corps

CHARACTER OF SEPARATION | REPORT OF SEPARATION FROM THE ARMED FORCES OF THE UNITED STATES | DEPARTMENT **AIR FORCE**

HONORABLE

1. LAST NAME — FIRST NAME — MIDDLE NAME **BRADSHAW, FRANK BERT JR.** | 2. SERVICE NUMBER **AO 2 218 619** | 3. GRADE — RATE — RANK AND DATE OF APPOINTMENT **1st Lt 5 Feb 53** | 4. COMPONENT AND BRANCH OR CLASS **USAF**

5. QUALIFICATIONS

SPECIALTY NUMBER OR SYMBOL **3254** | RELATED CIVILIAN OCCUPATION AND D. O. T. NUMBER **Chemical Engineer 0-15.01** | 6. EFFECTIVE DATE OF SEPARATION DAY **27** MONTH **Aug** YEAR **'53** | 7. TYPE OF SEPARATION **Release from Active Duty**

8. REASON AND AUTHORITY FOR SEPARATION **Conv of the Govt — Sec 513, PL 381-80th Congress & msg Hq USAF AFPMP-4 ALMAJCOM 708753, dtd 31 Jul 53** | 9. PLACE OF SEPARATION **Manzano Base, Albuquerque, New Mexico**

10. DATE OF BIRTH DAY **15** MONTH **Sep** YEAR **26** | 11. PLACE OF BIRTH (City and State) **Memphis, Tennessee** | 12. DESCRIPTION SEX **Male** RACE **Cau** COLOR HAIR **Brown** COLOR EYES **Blue** HEIGHT **6' 0"** WEIGHT **180**

13. REGISTERED YES / NO **Not Applicable** SELECTIVE SERVICE NUMBER | 14. SELECTIVE SERVICE LOCAL BOARD NUMBER (City, County, State) **Not Applicable** | 15. INDUCTED DAY MONTH **N/A** YEAR

16. ENLISTED IN OR TRANSFERRED TO A RESERVE COMPONENT YES / NO COMPONENT AND BRANCH OR CLASS **Not Applicable** | COGNIZANT DISTRICT OR AREA COMMAND **Not Applicable**

17. MEANS OF ENTRY OTHER THAN BY INDUCTION ☐ ENLISTED ☐ REENLISTED ☒ COMMISSIONED ☐ CALLED FROM INACTIVE DUTY | 18. GRADE — RATE OR RANK AT TIME OF ENTRY INTO ACTIVE SERVICE **2nd Lt**

19. DATE AND PLACE OF ENTRY INTO ACTIVE SERVICE DAY **22** MONTH **Jun** YEAR **51** PLACE (City and State) **San Antonio, Texas** | 20. HOME ADDRESS AT TIME OF ENTRY INTO ACTIVE SERVICE (St., R.F.D., City, County and State) **Columbia, South Carolina**

STATEMENT OF SERVICE FOR PAY PURPOSES | A. YEARS | B. MONTHS | C. DAYS | 21. ENLISTMENT ALLOWANCE PAID ON EXTENSION OF ENLISTMENT, IF ANY

21. NET (**N/A**) SERVICE COMPLETED FOR PAY PURPOSES EXCLUDING THIS PERIOD | 0 | 0 | 0 | DAY MONTH YEAR AMOUNT

22. NET SERVICE COMPLETED FOR PAY PURPOSES THIS PERIOD | 2 | 2 | 6 | **Not Applicable**

23. OTHER SERVICE (Act of 16 June 1942 as amended) COMPLETED FOR PAY PURPOSES | 0 | 6 | 24 | 26. FOREIGN AND/OR SEA SERVICE YEARS MONTHS DAYS **None**

24. TOTAL NET SERVICE COMPLETED FOR PAY PURPOSES | 2 | 9 | 0

27. DECORATIONS, MEDALS, BADGES, COMMENDATIONS, CITATIONS AND CAMPAIGN RIBBONS AWARDED OR AUTHORIZED **None**

28. MOST SIGNIFICANT DUTY ASSIGNMENT **Electrical Officer** | 29. WOUNDS RECEIVED AS A RESULT OF ACTION WITH ENEMY FORCES (Place and date, if known) **None**

30. SERVICE SCHOOLS OR COLLEGES, COLLEGE TRAINING COURSES AND/OR POST-GRAD. COURSES SUCCESSFULLY COMPLETED **None** | DATES (From–To) | MAJOR COURSES | 31. SERVICE TRAINING COURSES SUCCESSFULLY COMPLETED **USAF OCS 1951 Ph 1, Elect Fund 195? Special Weapons 1952**

MOPS200.00 pda/c of E. LEVIN LT. COL. FC 215670

32A. KIND & AMT. OF INSURANCE & MTHLY PREMIUM **NSLI 10,000** | 32B. INSURANCE IN FORCE PRIOR TO 28 APRIL ☒ YES ☐ NO ☐ UNKNOWN **Waiver PL 23** | 33. MONTH ALLOTMENT DISCONTINUED | 34. MONTH NEXT PREMIUM DUE **N/A**

35. TOTAL PAYMENT UPON SEPARATION **$272.28** | 36. TRAVEL OR MILEAGE ALLOWANCE INCLUDED IN TOTAL PAYMENT **$109.02** | 37. DISBURSING OFFICER'S NAME AND SYMBOL NUMBER **E. LEVIN LT. COL. FC 215670**

38. REMARKS (Continue on reverse) **F/P pd DOV# 700246 . 700381 .**
DD FORM 217 AF ISSUED BLOOD GROUP "A" AUTH LUMP SUM PAYMENT FOR FORTY (40) DAYS UNUSED ACC LV | 39. SIGNATURE OF OFFICER AUTHORIZED TO SIGN *James M Pumford* NAME, GRADE AND TITLE (Typed) **JAMES M PUMFORD, CAPTAIN PERSONNEL OFFICER**

40. V A BENEFITS PREVIOUSLY APPLIED FOR (Specify type) COMPENSATION, PENSION, INSURANCE BENEFITS, ETC **Not Applicable** | CLAIM NUMBER **Not Applicable**

41. DATES OF LAST CIVILIAN EMPLOYMENT FROM **None** TO **None** | 42. MAIN CIVILIAN OCCUPATION **None** | 43. NAME AND ADDRESS OF LAST CIVILIAN EMPLOYER **None**

44. UNITED STATES CITIZEN ☒ YES ☐ NO | 45. MARITAL STATUS **Single** | NON-SERVICE EDUCATION (Years successfully completed) GRAM MAR **8** HIGH SCHOOL **4** COL LEGE **5** DEGREE(S) **BCE** | MAJOR COURSE OR FIELD **Civil Engineer**

47. PERMANENT ADDRESS FOR MAILING PURPOSES AFTER SEPARATION (St., R.F.D., City, County and State) **406 S. Perkins Road Memphis, Tennessee** | 48. SIGNATURE OF PERSON BEING SEPARATED *Frank B Bradshaw, Jr.*

DD FORM 214 JUL 52 EDITION OF 1 JAN 50 IS OBSOLETE. INDIVIDUAL'S COPY (TO BE DELIVERED TO THE INDIVIDUAL BEING SEPARATED) | 1

(2) DD214—Official US government service record showing Frank Bradshaw's service in the Special Weapons Command at Manzano Base, August 27, 1953

CORNELL UNIVERSITY
ITHACA, NEW YORK

OFFICE OF ADMISSIONS

August 15, 1947

Mr. Frank B. Bradshaw, Jr.
Box 92, Rt. #5, Perkins Ave.
Memphis, Tennessee

Dear Mr. Bradshaw:

I am happy to inform you that your application for
admission in September 1947 to the School of Civil
Engineering at Cornell University has been approved. You
will be admitted at that time providing that you meet the
following requirements: the deposit of twenty-five dollars
and the vaccination certificate. Necessary forms are
inclosed.

This approval is for entrance in the Fall of 1947 only.
If anything should arise to prevent your matriculation at
that time, we will appreciate prompt notification so that
someone else may have the opportunity which has now been
assigned to you.

Registration Forms will be mailed to you at a later date,
provided you meet the above requirements.

Very truly yours,

Herbert H. Williams
Director of Admissions

vm
Inc.

(3) Cornell University Acceptance Letter, August 15, 1947

The Senior Class
of
Cornell University
announces its

Eighty-second Annual Commencement

Monday, June twelfth

Nineteen hundred and fifty

Ithaca, New York

Bachelors of Architecture

Shirley Jene Kerr....................1265 Shady Ave., Pitts., Pa.
Daniel Sharpe Kilby..............1530 Tenn. St., Lawrence, Kan.
George Franklin Kimmell..........197 Fort Ave., Keymed, W. Va.
Louis Andre Lamoraux, jr........167 Euclid Ave., Mansfield, Ohio
Ralph Mignone....................103 Hull St., Brooklyn, N. Y.
Leopold Solomon Moscowitz.......4325-47th St., L. I. C., N. Y.
Robert Grant Neiley................527 Paen St., Endicott, N. Y.
Willard Charles Pistler, jr.....Crest View Orchard L., Cinncinnati 13, O.
Walter Alan Rutes..............849 Linden Blvd., Brooklyn, N. Y.
David George Smith...........312 Central Ave., Fredonia, N. Y.
Philip Blacher Stalnman........80 Hatfield Pl., Staten Island, N. Y
John Joseph Tewhill, jr.....40 Trumbull Ave., Northampton, Mass.
William Gregory Tracy.....620 San Marco Dr., Ft. Lauderdale, Fla.
Walter Benjamin Van Gelder..4845 Hutchins Pl., Washington 7, D. C.
Robert John Von Dohlen..........989 Lorimer St., Brooklyn, N. Y.
James Wilson Yarnell..........177 St. Andrews, Charlestown, S. C.

Bachelors of Fine Arts

Phyllis A. Fein.............12 Seaman Rd., Poughkeepsie, N. Y.
Bernice June Flint...........22 Alps Rd., Mountain View, WW.ST.
Kenneth Melvin Lansing..........12 Palmer St., Stillwater, N. Y.
Frederic Cabot Lyford..............19 Ross Rd., Scarsdale, N. Y.
Harry Douglas Semonin, jr..............Box 207, Miami, Florida
Elizabeth Middleton Severinghaus....Haverford School, Haverford, Pa.

Bachelors of Civil Engineering

Bertram Gibson Ahearn........158 Burns Sr., Forest Hills, N. Y.
Edward Pierce Arbogast, II....................Pearl River, N. Y.
William Joseph Bartels......131 Calighi Ave., New Rochelle, N. Y.
Charles Robert Bauerlein....651 Tompkins Ave., Staten Island, N. Y.
Frank Bert Bradshaw, jr........4065 Perkins Rd., Memphis, Tenn.
Roger DeGrout Brown........840 College Ave., Niagara Falls, N. Y.
Floyd Ray Cannon............................RR 2, Newton, Iowa
Seleck John Carpenter........85 Cassing Ave., Eggertsville, N. Y.
Ronald Squire Clark............11 Letchworth St., Auburn, N. Y.
John Foster Coffin, III.........Willard Straight Hall, Ithaca, N. Y

(4) Cornell University Graduation Program, June 12, 1950

Made in the USA
Middletown, DE
04 January 2022